THE COMPLETE
HEART HEALTHY COOKBOOK

"Crispy and Delicious Heart-Healthy

Recipes for your Taste Buds"

ALLIE NAGEL

Copyright © 2024 by Allie Nagel

DISCLAIMER

This cookbook is intended to provide general information and recipes.

The recipes provided in this cookbook are not intended to replace or be a substitute for medical advice from a physician.

The reader should consult a healthcare professional for any specific medical advice, diagnosis or treatment.

Any specific dietary advice provided in this cookbook is not intended to replace or be a substitute for medical advice from a physician.

The author is not responsible or liable for any adverse effects experienced by readers of this cookbook as a result of following the recipes or dietary advice provided.

The author makes no representations or warranties of any kind (express or implied) as to the accuracy, completeness, reliability or suitability of the recipes provided in this cookbook.

The author disclaims any and all liability for any damages arising out of the use or misuse of the recipes provided in this cookbook. The reader must also take care to ensure that the recipes provided in this cookbook are prepared and cooked safely.

The recipes provided in this cookbook are for informational purposes only and should not be used as a substitute for professional medical advice, diagnosis or treatment.

TABLE OF CONTENTS

INTRODUCTION

A heart-healthy diet plays a pivotal role in maintaining cardiovascular well-being and preventing heart-related diseases.

Focused on nourishing the heart and circulatory system, this dietary approach emphasizes nutrient-rich foods that contribute to optimal heart function.

The cornerstone of such a diet is a variety of colorful fruits and vegetables, which provide essential vitamins, minerals, and antioxidants that combat inflammation and oxidative stress, key contributors to heart disease.

Whole grains, such as brown rice, quinoa, and oats, are integral components of a heart-healthy diet, as they deliver fiber that helps manage cholesterol levels and promote your overall heart health.

Lean proteins, including fish rich in omega-3 fatty acids, skinless poultry, legumes, and nuts, offer a balance of essential amino acids and healthy fats.

Omega-3 fatty acids, in particular, play a crucial role in reducing the risk of coronary artery disease and maintaining a steady heartbeat.

Limiting saturated and trans fats is essential for heart health. Foods high in these fats, such as red meat and processed snacks, can elevate cholesterol levels and contribute to arterial plaque formation.

Instead, opting for healthier fat sources like olive oil, avocados, and nuts promotes a favorable lipid profile.

Managing sodium intake is another key aspect of a heart-healthy diet.

Choosing fresh, whole foods over processed options, and using herbs and spices for flavor instead of salt, can help maintain a balanced sodium intake.

Finally, making mindful choices in food selection and adopting a balanced approach can significantly contribute to a heart-healthy lifestyle and mitigate the risk of cardiovascular diseases.

CHAPTER 1

BENEFITS OF USING AN AIR FRYER

1. **Healthier Cooking:** Air fryers use hot air circulation to cook food, requiring minimal or no oil. This results in lower fat content compared to traditional frying methods, making it a healthier cooking option.

2. **Reduced Fat Intake:** With significantly less oil needed, air frying helps reduce overall fat consumption, which is beneficial for those looking to manage their weight and cholesterol levels.

3. **Lower Calorie Content:** Since less oil is used, the calorie content of air-fried foods is generally lower than their traditionally fried counterparts, making it a great option for those watching their calorie intake.

4. **Versatility:** Air fryers can cook a variety of foods, from vegetables and meats to desserts. This versatility allows for a wide range of meal options without sacrificing taste or texture.

5. **Faster Cooking Times:** Air fryers typically cook food faster than traditional methods. This can be

advantageous for busy individuals looking to prepare meals quickly.

6. **Energy Efficiency:** Air fryers are generally more energy-efficient than traditional ovens, as they require less time and energy to reach cooking temperatures.

7. **Less Odor:** The enclosed cooking chamber of an air fryer helps contain cooking smells, preventing strong odors from spreading throughout the kitchen.

8. **Ease of Use:** Air fryers are user-friendly with simple controls, making them accessible to individuals of all cooking skill levels.

9. **Easy Cleanup:** Many air fryer components are dishwasher-safe, simplifying the cleaning process and reducing the time spent on post-cooking cleanup.

10. **Crispy Texture:** Air fryers produce a crispy exterior on foods, similar to traditional frying, providing a satisfying texture without the excess oil.

11. **Preservation of Nutrients:** The quick cooking process in an air fryer helps retain more nutrients in food compared to longer cooking times or boiling.

12. **No Preheating Required:** Air fryers often eliminate the need for preheating, saving time and energy during meal preparation.

13. **Safe Cooking Environment:** The closed cooking chamber minimizes the risk of splattering hot oil, reducing the likelihood of burns or accidents in the kitchen.

14. **Cooking for Dietary Restrictions:** Air frying allows for the preparation of dishes suitable for various dietary restrictions, including gluten-free and vegan options.

15. **Convenient for Small Spaces:** Air fryers are compact appliances, making them suitable for small kitchens or spaces where a traditional oven might not be practical.

LOW-FAT COOKING TECHNIQUES FOR HEART HEALTH

1. **Grilling:** Grilling is a low-fat cooking technique that imparts a delicious smoky flavor to food without the need for excessive amounts of added fats. Lean

meats, poultry, and vegetables are excellent choices for grilling.

2. **Baking:** Baking involves cooking food in an oven without the need for frying in oil. It's a versatile method suitable for proteins like chicken or fish, as well as vegetables and even desserts.

3. **Steaming:** Steaming involves cooking food over boiling water, preserving nutrients and flavors without the need for added fats. It's an excellent method for cooking vegetables, fish, and dumplings.

4. **Poaching:** Poaching involves gently simmering food in liquid, usually water or broth. This method is commonly used for delicate proteins like fish or eggs, requiring minimal added fats.

5. **Broiling:** Broiling exposes food to high heat from above, allowing fats to drip away. It's a quick cooking method suitable for lean cuts of meat and vegetables.

6. **Roasting:** Roasting involves cooking food in an oven using dry heat. It's a great method for vegetables, and by using minimal oil, you can achieve a crispy texture without excess fat.

7. **Sautéing with Minimal Oil:** Sautéing is a quick cooking method that uses a small amount of oil or cooking spray. By keeping the oil quantity low, you can still achieve great flavors with reduced fat content.

8. **Slow Cooking:** Slow cooking allows for long, gentle cooking over low heat. It's suitable for lean meats, beans, and vegetables, resulting in tender dishes without excessive fat.

9. **Pressure Cooking:** Pressure cooking involves cooking food quickly under steam pressure. It's an efficient method for reducing cooking time and preserving nutrients without the need for added fats.

10. **Microwaving:** Microwaving is a quick and convenient way to cook food without the need for added fats. It's particularly suitable for vegetables, grains, and proteins.

11. **Broths and Stocks:** Cooking with flavorful broths or stocks can add moisture and taste to dishes without the need for excessive fats. This is common in poaching or braising.

12. **Marinating:** Marinating proteins in flavorful, low-fat liquids before cooking can enhance taste and tenderness without relying on added fats during the cooking process.

13. **Stir-Frying with Minimal Oil:** Stir-frying involves quickly cooking small, uniform pieces of food in a pan. By using minimal oil and incorporating plenty of vegetables, it can be a low-fat cooking option.

14. **Griddling:** Griddling involves cooking food on a flat surface, often without the need for added fats. It's suitable for items like pancakes, lean meats, and vegetables.

15. **Vinegar and Citrus:** Using vinegar or citrus juices as a base for marinades, dressings, or poaching liquids can add flavor without relying on excessive amounts of oil or fats.

EFFECTIVE EXERCISES FOR IMPROVED HEART HEALTH

1. **Brisk Walking:** A simple and accessible exercise, brisk walking elevates the heart rate, improves circulation, and helps maintain a healthy weight.

2. **Jogging or Running:** Running engages large muscle groups, enhancing cardiovascular endurance and promoting heart health. Start at a comfortable pace and gradually increase intensity as fitness improves.

3. **Cycling:** Whether on a stationary bike or outdoors, cycling is a low-impact exercise that strengthens the heart and lower body. It's suitable for various fitness levels.

4. **Swimming:** Swimming is a full-body workout that enhances cardiovascular fitness while being gentle on the joints. It improves endurance, strength, and flexibility.

5. **Jump Rope:** Jumping rope is an excellent cardiovascular exercise that improves coordination and agility. It's an efficient way to boost heart health with minimal equipment.

6. **High-Intensity Interval Training (HIIT):** HIIT involves short bursts of intense exercise followed by rest periods. It's a time-efficient way to improve cardiovascular fitness, burn calories, and enhance heart health.

7. **Rowing:** Rowing engages both upper and lower body muscles, providing a comprehensive cardiovascular workout. It also helps improve posture and strength.

8. **Elliptical Training:** Using an elliptical machine offers a low-impact alternative to running while providing an effective cardiovascular workout. It targets both the upper and lower body.

9. **Dancing:** Dancing is a fun and social way to boost heart health. Whether taking a dance class or simply dancing at home, it improves cardiovascular fitness and coordination.

10. **Aerobic Classes:** Participating in aerobic classes, such as step aerobics or dance aerobics, provides a structured and energetic cardiovascular workout.

11. **Stair Climbing:** Climbing stairs engages major muscle groups, elevates heart rate, and improves cardiovascular endurance. It's an effective and easily scalable exercise.

12. **Resistance Training:** Incorporating strength training exercises, such as weightlifting, enhances overall fitness and can contribute to improved heart

health by building muscle and increasing metabolism.

13. **Yoga:** While often associated with flexibility and relaxation, certain yoga styles incorporate dynamic movements that elevate heart rate, promoting cardiovascular health.

14. **Pilates:** Pilates focuses on core strength and flexibility but can also include cardiovascular components, particularly in more dynamic routines.

15. **Kickboxing:** Kickboxing workouts combine aerobic exercises with strength training, providing a high-energy, full-body workout that contributes to improved cardiovascular fitness.

FOODS TO EAT AND FOODS AVOID ON A HEART HEALTHY DIET

FOODS TO EAT

1. **Salmon:** Rich in omega-3 fatty acids, salmon supports heart health by reducing inflammation and improving cholesterol levels. It's also a good source of protein.

2. **Berries:** Blueberries, strawberries, and raspberries are packed with antioxidants, vitamins, and fiber, promoting heart health and reducing the risk of cardiovascular diseases.

3. **Oats:** High in soluble fiber, oats help lower cholesterol levels. They also provide sustained energy and can contribute to weight management.

4. **Leafy Greens:** Spinach, kale, and Swiss chard are rich in vitamins, minerals, and antioxidants. Their high fiber content supports heart health and helps regulate blood pressure.

5. **Avocado:** Avocados are a source of monounsaturated fats, which can help lower bad cholesterol. They also provide potassium, which supports heart function.

6. **Nuts:** Almonds, walnuts, and pistachios are heart-healthy snacks. They contain omega-3 fatty acids, fiber, and unsaturated fats that support cardiovascular health.

7. **Legumes:** Beans, lentils, and chickpeas are excellent sources of soluble fiber, protein, and nutrients.

8. **Olive Oil:** Rich in monounsaturated fats and antioxidants, olive oil supports heart health by

improving cholesterol levels and reducing inflammation.

9. **Flaxseeds:** Flaxseeds are high in omega-3 fatty acids, fiber, and lignans.

10. **Tomatoes:** Tomatoes contain lycopene, an antioxidant linked to heart health. They are also rich in vitamins and minerals, supporting overall well-being.

11. **Fatty Fish:** Besides salmon, other fatty fish like mackerel and trout are rich in omega-3 fatty acids, which are essential for heart health.

12. **Dark Chocolate:** Dark chocolate, in moderation, contains flavonoids that may improve heart health by reducing blood pressure and improving blood flow.

13. **Whole Grains:** Brown rice, quinoa, and whole wheat provide complex carbohydrates and fiber, promoting heart health and helping with weight management.

FOODS TO AVOID

1. **Trans Fats:** Found in many processed and fried foods, trans fats increase bad cholesterol (LDL) and

decrease good cholesterol (HDL), contributing to heart disease. Avoid items with partially hydrogenated oils on the ingredient list.

2. **Saturated Fats:** High intake of saturated fats, found in red meat, full-fat dairy products, and certain oils, can raise cholesterol levels. Opt. for lean meats and low-fat dairy to reduce saturated fat intake.

3. **Processed Meats:** Processed meats like sausages, hot dogs, and bacon often contain high levels of sodium and unhealthy fats. Their consumption is linked to an increased risk of heart disease.

4. **Excessive Salt:** High sodium intake can lead to hypertension and increase the risk of heart problems. Limit processed and packaged foods, and opt for fresh, whole foods with natural flavors.

5. **Added Sugars:** Excessive sugar intake contributes to obesity and diabetes, increasing the risk of heart disease. Avoid sugary drinks, candies, and processed foods with hidden sugars.

6. **Sugar-Sweetened Beverages:** Regular consumption of sugary drinks is associated with weight gain and

an elevated risk of heart disease. Choose water, herbal teas, or unsweetened beverages instead.

7. **Highly Processed Foods:** Many processed foods contain unhealthy fats, sodium, and added sugars. Opt. for whole, minimally processed foods to support heart health.

8. **Fast Food:** Fast food is often high in unhealthy fats, sodium, and calories. Frequent consumption is linked to obesity and heart disease. Choose homemade or healthier restaurant options.

9. **Canned Soups and Broths:** Canned soups often contain high levels of sodium, which can contribute to hypertension. Choose low-sodium or homemade alternatives.

10. **Commercially Baked Goods:** Many baked goods, such as cookies, cakes, and pastries, are high in trans fats, sugar, and refined flour. Opt. for homemade or choose healthier alternatives.

11. **Deep-Fried Foods:** Fried foods, like French fries and fried chicken, are high in unhealthy fats and calories. Choose baked, grilled, or air-fried options for a heart-healthy alternative.

12. **Full-Fat Dairy:** Whole-fat dairy products contain saturated fats that can raise cholesterol levels. Choose low-fat or fat-free options for dairy consumption.

13. **Shellfish High in Cholesterol:** While seafood is generally heart-healthy, some shellfish, such as shrimp, can be high in cholesterol. Consume them in moderation.

14. Certain Cooking Oils: Limit the use of oils high in saturated fats, such as palm oil and coconut oil.

15. Highly Caffeinated or Sugary Energy Drinks: These beverages often contain excessive caffeine and added sugars, leading to potential heart health issues. Choose water, herbal teas, or other low-calorie options.

CHAPTER 2

14-DAY MEAL PLAN

DAY 1

Breakfast: Air-Fried Oatmeal Muffins

Lunch: Air-Fried Spicy Cauliflower Bites

Dinner: Air-Fried Salmon with Lemon and Dill

DAY 2

Breakfast: Air-Fried Sweet Potato Hash Browns

Lunch: Air-Fried Broccoli Tots

Dinner: Air-Fried Chicken Breast with Herbs

DAY 3

Breakfast: Air-Fried Apple Cinnamon Pancakes

Lunch: Air-Fried Mediterranean Stuffed Mushrooms

Dinner: Air-Fried Turkey Burgers

DAY 4

Breakfast: Air-Fried Mediterranean Egg Cups

Lunch: Air-Fried Garlic Parmesan Chicken Wings

Dinner: Air-Fried Shrimp Skewers

DAY 5

Breakfast: Air-Fried Banana Walnut Bread

Lunch: Air-Fried Salmon Patties

Dinner: Air-Fried Brussels Sprouts with Balsamic Glaze

DAY 6

Breakfast: Air-Fried Spinach and Feta Breakfast Wrap

Lunch: Air-Fried Quinoa and Vegetable Stuffed Peppers

Dinner: Air-Fried Cod with Garlic and Paprika

DAY 7

Breakfast: Air-Fried Blueberry Almond Oat Bars

Lunch: Air-Fried Turkey and Vegetable Meatballs

Dinner: Air-Fried Sweet Potato Fries

DAY 8

Breakfast: Air-Fried Cinnamon Raisin Bagel Chips

Lunch: Air-Fried Sweet Potato Wedges

Dinner: Air-Fried Quinoa Patties

DAY 9

Breakfast: Air-Fried Vegetable Frittata

Lunch: Air-Fried Lemon Garlic Shrimp

Dinner: Air-Fried Teriyaki Tofu

DAY 10

Breakfast: Air-Fried Salmon and Asparagus Breakfast Bundles

Lunch: Air-Fried Chickpea and Spinach Fritters

Dinner: Air-Fried Zucchini Chips

DAY 11

Breakfast: Air-Fried Oatmeal Muffins

Lunch: Air-Fried Spicy Cauliflower Bites

Dinner: Air-Fried Salmon with Lemon and Dill

DAY 12

Breakfast: Air-Fried Sweet Potato Hash Browns

Lunch: Air-Fried Broccoli Tots

Dinner: Air-Fried Chicken Breast with Herbs

DAY 13

Breakfast: Air-Fried Apple Cinnamon Pancakes

Lunch: Air-Fried Mediterranean Stuffed Mushrooms

Dinner: Air-Fried Turkey Burgers

DAY 14

Breakfast: Air-Fried Mediterranean Egg Cups

Lunch: Air-Fried Garlic Parmesan Chicken Wings

Dinner: Air-Fried Shrimp Skewers

CHAPTER 3

40 NUTRITIOUS RECIPES FOR A HEART HEALTHY DIET

BREAKFAST

Air-Fried Oatmeal Muffins

Preparation Time: 20 minutes

Serves: 12 muffins

Calories: 120 **Fat:** 4g **Sodium:** 5mg **Sugars:** 4g

Ingredients:

2 cups rolled oats

1 cup unsweetened almond milk

2 ripe bananas, mashed

1/2 cup unsweetened applesauce

1 teaspoon vanilla extract

1 teaspoon baking powder

1/2 teaspoon cinnamon

1/4 cup chopped nuts (e.g., walnuts or almonds, unsalted)

Cooking spray (for greasing)

Method of Preparation:

1. In a bowl, combine rolled oats, almond milk, mashed bananas, applesauce, vanilla extract, baking powder, and cinnamon.
2. Mix well.
3. Gently fold in chopped nuts into the mixture.
4. Preheat your air fryer to 350°F (180°C).
5. Grease muffin cups with cooking spray or use silicone muffin liners.
6. Spoon the oatmeal mixture into the muffin cups, filling each about two-thirds full.
7. Place the muffin cups in the air fryer basket, ensuring there's space between each.
8. Air fry for 12-15 minutes or until the muffins are set and slightly golden.
9. Allow the muffins to cool before removing them from the cups.

Air-Fried Sweet Potato Hash Browns

Preparation Time: 20 minutes

Serves: 4

Calories: 150 **Fat:** 4g **Carbs:** 28g **Protein:** 2g

Ingredients:

2 large sweet potatoes, peeled and grated

1 tablespoon olive oil

1/4 cup whole wheat flour

1 teaspoon baking powder

1/2 teaspoon black pepper

1/2 teaspoon paprika

1/4 cup finely chopped green onions

Cooking spray

Method of Preparation:

1. Preheat your air fryer to 375°F (190°C).

2. In a large bowl, combine grated sweet potatoes, olive oil, whole wheat flour, baking powder, black pepper, paprika, and chopped green onions.

3. Mix well.

4. Form the mixture into small patties and place them in a single layer in the air fryer basket, ensuring they are not touching.

5. Lightly spray the hash browns with cooking spray.

6. Air fry for 12-15 minutes, flipping halfway through, until they are golden brown and crispy.

7. Remove from the air fryer and let them cool for a few minutes before Serves.

Air-Fried Apple Cinnamon Pancakes

Preparation Time: 15 minutes

Serves: 4

Calories: 180 **Fat:** 4g **Sodium:** 25mg **Sugars:** 8g

Ingredients:

1 cup whole wheat flour

1 teaspoon baking powder

1/2 teaspoon cinnamon

1/2 cup unsweetened applesauce

1/2 cup almond milk (unsweetened)

1 large egg

1 medium apple, peeled and grated

Cooking spray (for air fryer)

Method of Preparation:

1. In a mixing bowl, combine whole wheat flour, baking powder, and cinnamon.
2. Add applesauce, almond milk, and the egg to the dry ingredients.
3. Mix until just combined.
4. Fold in the grated apple into the batter.
5. Preheat your air fryer to 350°F (180°C).
6. Lightly coat the air fryer basket with cooking spray.
7. Spoon portions of the batter onto the air fryer basket, leaving space between each pancake.
8. Air-fry for 8-10 minutes, flipping the pancakes halfway through, until they are golden brown and cooked through.

Air-Fried Mediterranean Egg Cups

Preparation Time: 20 minutes

Serves: 6

Calories: 120 **Fat:** 8g **Sodium:** 150mg

Ingredients:

6 large eggs

1 cup cherry tomatoes, halved

1/2 cup baby spinach, chopped

1/4 cup black olives, sliced

1/4 cup feta cheese, crumbled

1 tablespoon fresh parsley, chopped

Cooking spray (preferably olive oil spray)

Method of Preparation:

1. Preheat your air fryer to 350°F (180°C).
2. In a bowl, whisk the eggs and then add tomatoes, spinach, olives, feta, and parsley. Mix well.
3. Coat the air fryer cups with cooking spray.

4. Pour the egg mixture into the cups, filling each about two-thirds full.

5. Place the cups in the air fryer basket and cook for 12-15 minutes until the eggs are set.

6. Allow them to cool slightly before Serves.

Air-Fried Banana Walnut Bread

Preparation Time: 10 minutes

Serves: 8

Calories: 180 **Fat:** 5g **Sodium:** 100mg **Sugars:** 8g

Ingredients:

2 cups whole wheat flour

1 teaspoon baking soda

1/2 teaspoon baking powder

1/2 cup unsweetened applesauce (replace oil)

1/4 cup unsweetened almond milk

3 ripe bananas, mashed

1/2 cup chopped walnuts

1 teaspoon vanilla extract

Method of Preparation:

1. In a large bowl, mix whole wheat flour, baking soda, and baking powder.
2. In a separate bowl, combine mashed bananas, applesauce, almond milk, vanilla extract, and chopped walnuts.
3. Add the wet ingredients to the dry ingredients and stir until just combined.
4. Pour the batter into an air fryer-safe pan or mold.
5. Preheat the air fryer to 320°F (160°C) and air-fry the banana bread for 25-30 minutes or until a toothpick inserted comes out clean.
6. Allow it to cool before slicing.

Air-Fried Spinach and Feta Breakfast Wrap

Preparation Time: 20 minutes

Serves: 4

Calories: 320 **Protein:** 16g **Fat:** 16g **Sodium:** 320mg

Ingredients:

4 whole-grain tortillas

2 cups fresh spinach, chopped

1 cup cherry tomatoes, halved

1 cup crumbled feta cheese (low-fat if available)

4 large eggs

1 tablespoon olive oil

1 teaspoon black pepper

1 teaspoon dried oregano

Cooking spray (for the air fryer)

Method of Preparation:

1. In a skillet, heat olive oil over medium heat.
2. Add chopped spinach and sauté until wilted.
3. In a bowl, whisk together eggs, black pepper, and dried oregano.
4. Pour the egg mixture into the skillet with spinach, and scramble until cooked through.

5. Lay out the tortillas and evenly distribute the scrambled eggs, cherry tomatoes, and crumbled feta cheese among them.
6. Fold each tortilla into a wrap.
7. Preheat your air fryer to 350°F (180°C).
8. Lightly spray the air fryer basket with cooking spray.
9. Place the wraps in the air fryer basket, ensuring they are not touching.
10. Air fry for 5-7 minutes or until the wraps are golden and crispy.

Air-Fried Blueberry Almond Oat Bars

Preparation Time: 10 minutes

Serves: 12 bars

Calories: 180 **Fat:** 10g **Sodium:** 0mg **Sugars:** 7g

Ingredients:

2 cups rolled oats

1 cup almonds, chopped

1 cup fresh blueberries

1/2 cup almond butter

1/4 cup honey

1/4 cup unsweetened applesauce

1 teaspoon vanilla extract

Method of Preparation:

1. In a large bowl, combine rolled oats, chopped almonds, and fresh blueberries.
2. In a separate bowl, mix almond butter, honey, applesauce, and vanilla extract until well combined.
3. Pour the wet mixture over the dry ingredients and stir until evenly coated.
4. Press the mixture into a greased air fryer-safe pan.
5. Air fry at 350°F (180°C) for 15-20 minutes until the edges are golden brown.
6. Allow the bars to cool before cutting into Serving.

Air-Fried Cinnamon Raisin Bagel Chips

Preparation Time: 8 minutes

Serves: 4

Calories: 150 **Fat:** 4g **Sodium:** 120mg **Sugars:** 7g

Ingredients:

2 whole-grain bagels, sliced thinly

1 tablespoon olive oil

1 teaspoon ground cinnamon

1/2 cup raisins

Method of Preparation:

1. Preheat your air fryer to 350°F (180°C).
2. In a bowl, toss bagel slices with olive oil, cinnamon, and raisins until well coated.
3. Place the bagel slices in a single layer in the air fryer basket.
4. Air fry for 5-7 minutes or until the chips are crispy and golden brown.
5. Allow them to cool before Serves.

Air-Fried Vegetable Frittata

Preparation Time: 10 minutes

Serves: 4

Calories: 180 **Protein:** 14g **Sugar:** 6g **Fat:** 11g

Ingredients:

6 large eggs

1 cup cherry tomatoes, halved

1 cup baby spinach, chopped

1/2 cup red bell pepper, diced

1/2 cup zucchini, diced

1/4 cup fresh basil, chopped

1/4 cup reduced-fat feta cheese, crumbled

1 teaspoon olive oil (for greasing)

Method of Preparation:

1. Preheat your air fryer to 350°F (180°C).
2. In a bowl, whisk the eggs until well beaten.
3. Add tomatoes, spinach, bell pepper, zucchini, basil, and feta cheese to the beaten eggs. Mix well.
4. Grease the air fryer basket with olive oil.
5. Pour the egg mixture into the basket and spread evenly.
6. Cook in the air fryer for 15-18 minutes or until the frittata is set and the top is golden brown.

7. Once done, carefully remove from the air fryer and let it cool for a few minutes before slicing.

Air-Fried Salmon and Asparagus Breakfast Bundles

Preparation Time: 15 minutes

Serves: 4

Calories: 250 **Protein:** 28g **Sugar:** 4g **Fat:** 14g

Ingredients:

4 salmon fillets (about 4 oz each)

1 bunch asparagus, trimmed

2 tablespoons olive oil

1 teaspoon lemon zest

1 teaspoon fresh thyme leaves

Pepper

Method of Preparation:

1. Preheat your air fryer to 400°F (200°C).

2. Place each salmon fillet on a piece of parchment paper.

3. Arrange asparagus spears beside each salmon fillet.

4. Drizzle olive oil over salmon and asparagus. Sprinkle with lemon zest, thyme and pepper.

5. Fold the parchment paper over the salmon and asparagus to create sealed bundles.

6. Place the bundles in the air fryer basket and cook for 10-12 minutes until the salmon is cooked through.

LUNCH

Air-Fried Spicy Cauliflower Bites

Preparation Time: 10 minutes

Serves: 4

Calories: 90 Fat: 7g Sodium: 25mg Sugars: 3

Ingredients:

1 medium-sized cauliflower, cut into florets

2 tablespoons olive oil

1 teaspoon smoked paprika

1 teaspoon garlic powder

1/2 teaspoon cayenne pepper (adjust to taste for spice)

Freshly ground black pepper to taste

Method of Preparation:

1. Preheat your air fryer to 375°F (190°C).
2. In a large bowl, toss cauliflower florets with olive oil, smoked paprika, garlic powder, cayenne pepper, and black pepper until evenly coated.
3. Place the seasoned cauliflower in the air fryer basket in a single layer, ensuring they are not overcrowded.
4. Air fry for 15-18 minutes, shaking the basket halfway through, until the cauliflower is golden brown and crispy.
5. Serve hot as a delicious and spicy appetizer.

Air-Fried Broccoli Tots

Preparation Time: 25 minutes

Serves: 4

Calories: 180 Sugars: 2g Fat: 13g Sodium: 25mg

Ingredients:

2 cups finely chopped broccoli

1 cup almond flour

2 flax eggs (2 tablespoons ground flaxseed + 6 tablespoons water)

1/4 cup nutritional yeast

1 teaspoon garlic powder

1 teaspoon onion powder

1/2 teaspoon black pepper

Cooking spray (for air frying)

Method of Preparation:

1. Preheat your air fryer to 375°F (190°C).
2. Steam the chopped broccoli until tender, then let it cool.
3. In a bowl, mix the almond flour, flax eggs, nutritional yeast, garlic powder, onion powder, and black pepper.
4. Add the cooled broccoli to the mixture and combine until it forms a dough.

5. Shape the mixture into tots and place them in the air fryer basket.

6. Lightly coat the tots with cooking spray.

7. Air fry for 15-18 minutes, turning halfway, until they are golden and crispy.

Air-Fried Mediterranean Stuffed Mushrooms

Preparation Time: 30 minutes

Serves: 4

Calories: 220 Sugars: 3g Fat: 12g Sodium: 180mg

Ingredients:

16 large mushrooms, stems removed and chopped

1 cup quinoa, cooked

1 cup cherry tomatoes, diced

1/2 cup Kalamata olives, chopped

1/4 cup red onion, finely diced

2 cloves garlic, minced

2 tablespoons olive oil

1 teaspoon dried oregano

1/2 teaspoon black pepper

Cooking spray (for air frying)

Method of Preparation:

1. Preheat your air fryer to 375°F (190°C).

2. In a pan, sauté chopped mushroom stems, garlic, and red onion in olive oil until softened.

3. In a bowl, combine the sautéed mixture with cooked quinoa, cherry tomatoes, olives, oregano, and black pepper.

4. Stuff each mushroom cap with the quinoa mixture.

5. Place stuffed mushrooms in the air fryer basket, lightly coat with cooking spray.

6. Air fry for 12-15 minutes until mushrooms are tender.

Air-Fried Garlic Parmesan Chicken Wings

Preparation Time: 35 minutes

Serves: 4

Calories: 320 Protein: 28g Carbs: 2g Fat: 22g

Ingredients:

2 lbs. chicken wings, tips removed

2 tablespoons olive oil

4 cloves garlic, minced

1/2 cup grated Parmesan cheese

1 teaspoon dried oregano

1 teaspoon dried basil

1/2 teaspoon black pepper

1 tablespoon lemon juice

Fresh parsley for garnish

Method of Preparation:

1. Preheat your air fryer to 400°F (200°C).

2. In a large bowl, toss the chicken wings with olive oil, minced garlic, Parmesan cheese, oregano, basil, black pepper, and lemon juice until well coated.

3. Place the wings in the air fryer basket, ensuring they are not overcrowded, and cook for 25-30 minutes, flipping halfway through, until golden and crispy.

4. Garnish with fresh parsley before Serves.

Air-Fried Salmon Patties

Preparation Time: 20 minutes

Serves: 4

Calories: 220 Protein: 26g Carbs: 5g Fat: 10g

Ingredients:

1 lb. fresh salmon, skinless and boneless

1/4 cup whole wheat breadcrumbs

1/4 cup chopped green onions

2 tablespoons chopped fresh dill

1 tablespoon Dijon mustard

1 egg, beaten

1 tablespoon olive oil

Lemon wedges for Serves

Method of Preparation:

1. Cut the salmon into small chunks and place in a food processor. Pulse until finely chopped.
2. In a bowl, combine the salmon, breadcrumbs, green onions, dill, Dijon mustard, and beaten egg.
3. Mix until well combined.
4. Divide the mixture into patties and place on a plate.
5. Preheat the air fryer to 375°F (190°C).
6. Brush the patties with olive oil and air-fry for 10-12 minutes, flipping halfway through, until golden brown and cooked through.
7. Serve with lemon wedges.

Air-Fried Quinoa and Vegetable Stuffed Peppers

Preparation Time: 40 minutes

Serves: 4

Calories: 220 42g Sugars: 5 Fat: 3g Sodium: 50mg

Ingredients:

4 large bell peppers, halved and seeds removed

1 cup quinoa, rinsed and drained

2 cups vegetable broth (low sodium)

1 cup cherry tomatoes, diced

1 cup zucchini, diced

1 cup mushrooms, diced

1 cup spinach, chopped

2 cloves garlic, minced

1 teaspoon dried oregano

1 teaspoon dried basil

1/2 teaspoon black pepper

Cooking spray (olive oil-based)

Method of Preparation:

1. Preheat the air fryer to 375°F (190°C).
2. In a medium saucepan, combine quinoa and vegetable broth. Bring to a boil, then reduce heat, cover, and simmer for 15-20 minutes, or until quinoa is cooked and liquid is absorbed.
3. In a large bowl, mix cooked quinoa, cherry tomatoes, zucchini, mushrooms, spinach, garlic, oregano, basil, and black pepper.
4. Stuff each bell pepper half with the quinoa and vegetable mixture.
5. Lightly coat the air fryer basket with cooking spray and place the stuffed peppers inside.
6. Air-fry for 15-20 minutes or until peppers are tender and slightly charred.

Air-Fried Turkey and Vegetable Meatballs

Preparation Time: 30 minutes

Serves: 4

Calories: 180 Sugars: 1g Fat: 8g Sodium: 60mg

Ingredients:

1 lb. ground turkey (lean)

1/2 cup rolled oats, finely ground

1/2 cup grated zucchini, squeezed to remove excess moisture

1/4 cup finely chopped onion

1/4 cup finely chopped bell pepper

2 cloves garlic, minced

1 teaspoon dried thyme

1 teaspoon dried rosemary

1/2 teaspoon black pepper

Cooking spray (olive oil-based)

Method of Preparation:

1. Preheat the air fryer to 375°F (190°C).

2. In a large bowl, combine ground turkey, ground oats, grated zucchini, onion, bell pepper, garlic, thyme, rosemary, and black pepper. Mix well.

3. Form the mixture into meatballs, 1 inch in diameter.

4. Lightly coat the air fryer basket with cooking spray and place the meatballs inside.

5. Air-fry for 15-18 minutes or until the meatballs are cooked through and browned.

Air-Fried Sweet Potato Wedges

Preparation Time: 50 minutes

Serves: 4

Calories: 120 Fat: 3g Sodium: 30mg Sugars: 4g

Ingredients:

3 medium sweet potatoes, washed and cut into wedges

1 tablespoon olive oil

1 teaspoon smoked paprika

1/2 teaspoon garlic powder

1/2 teaspoon onion powder

1/2 teaspoon ground black pepper

Fresh parsley for garnish (optional)

Method of Preparation:

1. Preheat your air fryer to 400°F (200°C).
2. In a large bowl, toss sweet potato wedges with olive oil, smoked paprika, garlic powder, onion powder, and black pepper until evenly coated.
3. Place the seasoned sweet potato wedges in the air fryer basket, making sure they are in a single layer for even cooking.
4. Air fry for 15-20 minutes or until the wedges are golden brown and crispy, shaking the basket halfway through to ensure even cooking.
5. Once done, remove from the air fryer and garnish with fresh parsley if desired.

Air-Fried Lemon Garlic Shrimp

Preparation Time: 25 minutes (including marination)

Serves: 4

Calories: 180 Fat: 9g Sugars: 0g Sodium: 10mg

Ingredients:

1-pound large shrimp, peeled and deveined

2 tablespoons olive oil

3 cloves garlic, minced

1 teaspoon lemon zest

2 tablespoons fresh lemon juice

1 teaspoon paprika

1/2 teaspoon black pepper

1/4 teaspoon cayenne pepper (optional for heat)

Fresh parsley, chopped (for garnish)

Method of Preparation:

1. In a bowl, combine olive oil, minced garlic, lemon zest, lemon juice, paprika, black pepper, and cayenne pepper (if using).
2. Add the peeled and deveined shrimp to the bowl, ensuring they are well-coated with the marinade.
3. Let it marinate for at least 15 minutes.
4. Preheat your air fryer to 375°F (190°C).

5. Place the marinated shrimp in the air fryer basket in a single layer, making sure they are not crowded.

6. Air-fry for 8-10 minutes, shaking the basket halfway through, until the shrimp are pink and cooked through.

7. Garnish with chopped fresh parsley before Serves.

Air-Fried Chickpea and Spinach Fritters

Preparation Time: 20 minutes

Serves: 4

Calories: 180 Fat: 6g Sodium: 20mg Sugars: 2g

Ingredients:

1 can (15 oz) chickpeas, drained and rinsed

2 cups fresh spinach, finely chopped

1/2 cup whole wheat flour

1 small onion, finely chopped

2 cloves garlic, minced

1 teaspoon cumin

1/2 teaspoon coriander

1/4 teaspoon black pepper

1/4 cup chopped fresh parsley

1 tablespoon olive oil (for mixture)

Cooking spray (for air frying)

Method of Preparation:

1. In a food processor, combine chickpeas, spinach, whole wheat flour, onion, garlic, cumin, coriander, and black pepper.
2. Pulse until well combined but not completely smooth.
3. Transfer the mixture to a bowl and stir in chopped parsley.
4. If the mixture is too dry, add a tablespoon of olive oil to moisten.
5. Preheat your air fryer to 375°F (190°C).
6. Form the mixture into golf ball-sized rounds and flatten slightly to create fritters.

7. Lightly coat the air fryer basket with cooking spray. Place the fritters in the basket, ensuring they are not touching.

8. Air fry for 12-15 minutes or until the fritters are golden brown and crispy, flipping halfway through the cooking time.

9. Serve warm with a side of your favorite heart-healthy dip or sauce.

DINNER

Air-Fried Salmon with Lemon and Dill

Preparation Time: 30 minutes

Serves: 4

Calories: 250 Protein: 30g Fat: 13g Carbs: 2g

Ingredients:

4 salmon fillets

1 tablespoon olive oil

1 lemon (juiced and zested)

2 tablespoons fresh dill (chopped)

1 teaspoon black pepper

Method of Preparation:

1. Preheat your air fryer to 375°F (190°C).
2. In a bowl, mix olive oil, lemon juice, lemon zest, chopped dill, and black pepper.
3. Place salmon fillets in a shallow dish and coat them with the lemon-dill mixture.
4. Let them marinate for 15 minutes.
5. Arrange the marinated salmon fillets in the air fryer basket, ensuring they are not overcrowded.
6. Air fry for 12-15 minutes, or until salmon is cooked through and easily flakes with a fork.
7. Serve immediately, garnished with additional fresh dill and lemon slices.

Air-Fried Chicken Breast with Herbs

Preparation Time: 25 minutes

Serves: 4

Calories: 220 Protein: 32g Fat: 9g Carbs: 1g

Ingredients:

4 boneless, skinless chicken breasts

2 tablespoons olive oil

1 tablespoon fresh rosemary (chopped)

1 tablespoon fresh thyme (chopped)

1 teaspoon garlic powder

1/2 teaspoon black pepper

Method of Preparation:

1. Preheat your air fryer to 400°F (200°C).
2. Rub chicken breasts with olive oil, chopped rosemary, thyme, garlic powder, and black pepper.
3. Place the seasoned chicken breasts in the air fryer basket, making sure they are not touching.
4. Air fry for 18-20 minutes, flipping halfway through, until the internal temperature reaches 165°F (74°C).
5. Let the chicken rest for a few minutes before slicing.

Air-Fried Turkey Burgers

Preparation Time: 25 minutes (including air frying)

Serves: 4

Calories: 220 Carbs: 18g Fat: 6g Sodium: 60mg

Ingredients:

1 lb. lean ground turkey

1/2 cup finely chopped onions

1/4 cup finely chopped bell peppers

2 cloves garlic, minced

1 tsp dried oregano

1 tsp dried thyme

1 tsp smoked paprika

Ground black pepper to taste

Whole wheat burger buns (for Serves)

Lettuce, tomato, and other preferred toppings

Method of Preparation:

1. In a bowl, combine ground turkey, onions, bell peppers, garlic, oregano, thyme, smoked paprika, and black pepper. Mix well.

2. Shape the mixture into burger patties.

3. Preheat your air fryer to 375°F (190°C).

4. Place the turkey patties in the air fryer basket, leaving space between each.

5. Air fry for 15-18 minutes or until the internal temperature reaches 165°F (74°C), flipping the patties halfway through.

6. Toast the whole wheat burger buns in the air fryer for 1-2 minutes.

7. Assemble the burgers with lettuce, tomato, and your preferred toppings.

Air-Fried Shrimp Skewers

Preparation Time: 25 minutes

Serves: 4

Calories: 150 Fat: 5g Sodium: 70mg Sugars: 0g

Ingredients:

1 lb. large shrimp, peeled and deveined

1 tablespoon olive oil

2 cloves garlic, minced

1 teaspoon paprika

1 teaspoon dried oregano

1 teaspoon ground black pepper

1 tablespoon fresh parsley, chopped

Wooden skewers, soaked in water

Method of Preparation:

1. In a bowl, mix olive oil, minced garlic, paprika, dried oregano, and ground black pepper.
2. Add the peeled and deveined shrimp to the bowl, coating them evenly with the spice mixture.
3. Marinate for 15 minutes.
4. Preheat your air fryer to 375°F (190°C).
5. Thread the marinated shrimp onto the soaked wooden skewers.
6. Place the skewers in the preheated air fryer basket, ensuring they are not crowded.
7. Air fry for 8-10 minutes, turning halfway through, until the shrimp are opaque and cooked through.
8. Sprinkle with fresh parsley before Serves.

Air-Fried Brussels Sprouts with Balsamic Glaze

Preparation Time: 25 minutes

Serves: 4

Calories: 90 Fat: 3g Sodium: 10mg Sugars: 4g

Ingredients:

1 lb. Brussels sprouts, trimmed and halved

2 tablespoons balsamic vinegar

1 tablespoon olive oil

1 teaspoon Dijon mustard

1 teaspoon honey (optional, for sweetness)

Freshly ground black pepper to taste

Method of Preparation:

1. Preheat the air fryer to 375°F (190°C).
2. In a bowl, whisk together balsamic vinegar, olive oil, Dijon mustard, and honey (if using).

3. Toss Brussels sprouts in the mixture until evenly coated.

4. Place Brussels sprouts in the air fryer basket, ensuring they are in a single layer.

5. Air fry for 15-20 minutes, shaking the basket halfway through, until the Brussels sprouts are crispy and golden.

6. Season with freshly ground black pepper to taste.

7. Serve immediately.

Air-Fried Cod with Garlic and Paprika

Preparation Time: 15 minutes

Serves: 4

Calories: 180 Fat: 8g Sodium: 60mg Sugars: 0g

Ingredients:

4 cod fillets

2 tablespoons olive oil

4 cloves garlic, minced

1 teaspoon smoked paprika

Freshly ground black pepper to taste

Method of Preparation:

1. Preheat the air fryer to 400°F (200°C).
2. Pat the cod fillets dry with a paper towel.
3. In a small bowl, mix together olive oil, minced garlic, smoked paprika, and black pepper.
4. Brush the cod fillets with the garlic and paprika mixture, ensuring they are well-coated.
5. Place cod fillets in the air fryer basket.
6. Air fry for 10-12 minutes until the cod is cooked through and flakes easily with a fork.
7. Serve immediately.

Air-Fried Sweet Potato Fries

Preparation Time: 25 minutes

Serves: 4

Calories: 120 Fat: 3g Sodium: 20mg Sugars: 5g

Ingredients:

2 large sweet potatoes, cut into fries

1 tablespoon olive oil

1 teaspoon paprika

1/2 teaspoon garlic powder

1/2 teaspoon onion powder

Freshly ground black pepper to taste

Method of Preparation:

1. Preheat the air fryer to 400°F (200°C).
2. In a large bowl, toss sweet potato fries with olive oil, paprika, garlic powder, onion powder, and black pepper.
3. Place the sweet potato fries in the air fryer basket.
4. Air fry for 15-20 minutes, shaking the basket halfway through, until the fries are crispy.
5. Serve immediately.

Air-Fried Quinoa Patties

Preparation Time: 30 minutes

Serves: 4

Calories: 220 Fat: 11g Sodium: 30mg Sugars: 2g

Ingredients:

2 cups cooked quinoa, cooled

1 cup finely chopped vegetables (e.g., bell peppers, onions, carrots)

2 tablespoons olive oil

2 eggs, beaten

1/2 teaspoon garlic powder

1/2 teaspoon cumin

Freshly ground black pepper to taste

Method of Preparation:

1. Preheat the air fryer to 375°F (190°C).
2. In a large bowl, mix together quinoa, chopped vegetables, olive oil, beaten eggs, garlic powder, cumin, and black pepper.
3. Form the mixture into patties.
4. Place the quinoa patties in the air fryer basket, ensuring they are not touching.

5. Air fry for 15-18 minutes, flipping the patties halfway through, until they are golden brown and crispy.
6. Serve immediately.

Air-Fried Teriyaki Tofu

Preparation Time: 30 minutes

Serves: 4

Calories: 160 Fat: 8g Sodium: 250mg Sugars: 5g

Ingredients:

1 block firm tofu, pressed and cubed

3 tablespoons low-sodium soy sauce

2 tablespoons rice vinegar

1 tablespoon maple syrup

1 teaspoon grated ginger

1 teaspoon minced garlic

1 tablespoon cornstarch (optional, for extra crispiness)

Method of Preparation:

1. Preheat the air fryer to 375°F (190°C).
2. In a bowl, whisk together soy sauce, rice vinegar, maple syrup, grated ginger, and minced garlic.
3. Toss the tofu cubes in the teriyaki sauce, ensuring they are well-coated.
4. If desired, coat tofu cubes in cornstarch for extra crispiness.
5. Place the tofu cubes in the air fryer basket.
6. Air fry for 20-25 minutes, shaking the basket halfway through, until the tofu is golden and crispy.
7. Serve immediately.

Air-Fried Zucchini Chips

Preparation Time: 20 minutes

Serves: 4

Calories: 70 Fat: 5g Sodium: 10mg Sugars: 3g

Ingredients:

2 medium zucchinis, thinly sliced

1 tablespoon olive oil

1/2 teaspoon garlic powder

1/2 teaspoon onion powder

1/2 teaspoon dried thyme

Freshly ground black pepper to taste

Method of Preparation:

1. Preheat the air fryer to 375°F (190°C).
2. In a bowl, toss zucchini slices with olive oil, garlic powder, onion powder, dried thyme, and black pepper.
3. Place the zucchini slices in the air fryer basket, ensuring they are in a single layer.
4. Air fry for 10-12 minutes, flipping the slices halfway through, until the zucchini chips are crispy.
5. Serve immediately.

DESSERTS

Air-Fried Cinnamon Apple Slices

Preparation Time: 15 minutes

Serves: 4

Calories: 120 **Protein:** 1g **Carbs:** 30g **Fat:** 2g

Ingredients:

4 medium apples, sliced

1 tablespoon cinnamon

1 tablespoon coconut oil

1 tablespoon honey (or alternative sweetener)

Method of Preparation:

1. Preheat the air fryer to 375°F (190°C).
2. In a bowl, toss apple slices with cinnamon and melted coconut oil.
3. Place coated apple slices in the air fryer basket.
4. Air fry for 8-10 minutes, shaking the basket halfway through.
5. Drizzle honey over the slices and air fry for an additional 2 minutes.
6. Serve warm.

Air-Fried Mango Coconut Tofu Bites

Preparation Time: 25 minutes

Serves: 3

Calories: 220 **Protein:** 10g **Carbs:** 15g **Fat:** 14g

Ingredients:

1 block firm tofu, cubed

1 cup mango chunks

2 tablespoons shredded coconut

1 tablespoon soy sauce

1 tablespoon olive oil

Method of Preparation:

1. Preheat the air fryer to 375°F (190°C).
2. In a bowl, mix tofu, mango chunks, shredded coconut, soy sauce, and olive oil.
3. Place the mixture in the air fryer basket.
4. Air fry for 15-20 minutes, shaking the basket occasionally.
5. Serve warm.

Air-Fried Baked Almond-Crusted Peaches

Preparation Time: 20 minutes

Serves: 4

Calories: 150 **Protein:** 3g **Carbs:** 20g **Fat:** 7g

Ingredients:

4 ripe peaches, halved

1/2 cup almond flour

2 tablespoons honey

1 teaspoon cinnamon

1 tablespoon coconut oil, melted

Method of Preparation:

1. Preheat the air fryer to 375°F (190°C).
2. In a bowl, combine almond flour, honey, cinnamon, and melted coconut oil.
3. Coat each peach half with the almond mixture.
4. Place the peaches in the air fryer basket.
5. Air fry for 12-15 minutes until golden and tender.

6. Serve warm.

Air-Fried Berry-Stuffed Puff Pastry

Preparation Time: 20 minutes

Serves: 4

Calories: 250 **Protein:** 5g **Carbs:** 35g **Fats:** 10g

Ingredients:

1 sheet puff pastry (preferably whole grain for added nutrition)

1 cup mixed berries (blueberries, raspberries, strawberries)

2 tablespoons honey

1 tablespoon chia seeds (high in omega-3s)

Method of Preparation:

1. Preheat your air fryer to 375°F (190°C).
2. Roll out the puff pastry and cut it into squares.
3. In a bowl, mix the berries, honey, and chia seeds.
4. Spoon the berry mixture onto the center of each puff pastry square.

5. Fold the pastry over the berries, forming a triangle, and press the edges to seal.

6. Place the stuffed pastries in the air fryer basket and cook for 12-15 minutes or until golden brown.

Air-Fried Almond Flour Blueberry Muffins

Preparation Time: 25 minutes

Serves: 12 muffins

Calories: 180 **Protein:** 6g **Carbs:** 10g **Fats:** 14g

Ingredients:

2 cups almond flour

1/4 cup coconut flour

1/2 teaspoon baking soda

3 large eggs

1/4 cup honey or maple syrup

1/3 cup coconut oil, melted

1 cup fresh blueberries

Method of Preparation:

1. Preheat your air fryer to 325°F (163°C).

2. In a bowl, whisk together almond flour, coconut flour and baking soda.

3. In another bowl, beat the eggs, then add honey and melted coconut oil.

4. Mix well.

5. Combine wet and dry ingredients, then gently fold in the blueberries.

6. Spoon the batter into muffin cups, filling each about 2/3 full.

7. Place the muffin cups in the air fryer basket and cook for 15-18 minutes or until a toothpick comes out clean.

CONCLUSION

In conclusion, this cookbook serves as a comprehensive guide to your culinary innovation, there by fostering your heart health through mindful and nutritious cooking.

Now that you've explored various recipes and techniques in this book, you would agree with me that the overarching theme revolves around embracing a heart-healthy lifestyle without compromising on flavor or satisfaction.

The benefits of using an air fryer for heart health are abundantly clear.

By minimizing the need for excessive oils and fats in your cooking, you will not only reduce the intake of unhealthy elements contributing to your heart disease but also create meals that are both delicious and nourishing.

The recipes created in this cookbook showcase the versatility of the air fryer.

Finally, remember that the emphasis on whole foods, lean proteins, and a spectrum of vibrant vegetables aligns seamlessly with the principles of a heart-healthy diet.

Printed in Great Britain
by Amazon

40353723R00046